Around
and
Around—
Love

Photographs by

Bob Adelman
Christa Armstrong
Alma Davenport Dailey
Bruce Davidson
Richard Erdoes
Laurence Fink
Jill Freedman
Ellen Galinsky
Burt Glinn
Hella Hammid
Charles Harbutt
Abigail Heyman
Ken Heyman
Chester Higgins, Jr.
Victor Laredo
Jan Lukas
Henry Margulies
Isabel Montero
Dorka Raynor
Bruce Roberts
Lee Romero
Jinx Roosevelt
Pat Ross
Hanna Schreiber
Sherry Suris
Suzanne Szasz
Burk Uzzle
Sandra Weiner

Around and Around— Love

by Betty Miles

Alfred A. Knopf ✦ New York

Photo Credits cover: Hella Hammid/Rapho. page 1: Hella Hammid/Rapho. page 2: Victor Laredo, top; Abigail Heyman/Magnum, bottom. page 3: Jan Lukas/Rapho, top; Suzanne Szasz, bottom. page 4: Chester Higgins, Jr./Rapho. page 5: Suzanne Szasz. page 6: Sherry Suris/Rapho. page 7: Hella Hammid/Rapho, top; Ken Heyman, bottom. page 8: Chester Higgins, Jr./Rapho. page 9: Jan Lukas/Rapho, top right; Burk Uzzle/Magnum, top left; Richard Erdoes, bottom. page 10: Ellen Galinsky. page 11: Henry Margulies. page 12: Ken Heyman, top; Jinx Roosevelt, bottom. page 13: Laurence Fink, top; Ellen Galinsky, bottom. page 14: Chester Higgins, Jr./Rapho, top; Jinx Roosevelt, bottom. page 15: Lee Romero. page 16: Henry Margulies, top; Jan Lukas/Rapho, bottom. page 17: Henry Margulies. page 18-19: Chester Higgins, Jr./Rapho. page 20: Burt Glinn/Magnum, top; Hanna Schreiber/Rapho, bottom. page 21: Chester Higgins, Jr./Rapho, top; Richard Erdoes, bottom. page 22-23: Ken Heyman. page 24: Hella Hammid/Rapho. page 25: Sandra Weiner, top; Laurence Fink, bottom. page 26: Hella Hammid/Rapho. page 27: Bruce Roberts/Rapho. page 28-29: Lee Romero. page 30: Ken Heyman. page 31: Abigail Heyman/Magnum, top; Jill Freedman/Photo Researchers, bottom. page 32: Abigail Heyman/Magnum. page 33: Dorka Raynor/Rapho, top right; Suzanne Szasz, middle; Bruce Davidson/Magnum, bottom. page 34: Chester Higgins, Jr./Rapho. page 35: Ken Heyman, top; Hella Hammid/Rapho, bottom. page 36: Charles Harbutt/Magnum, top; Ken Heyman, bottom. page 37: Isabel Montero, top; Alma Davenport Dailey, bottom. page 38: Bob Adelman/Magnum, top; Ellen Galinsky, bottom left; Lee Romero, bottom right. page 39: Suzanne Szasz, top; Christa Armstrong/Rapho, bottom. page 40: Hella Hammid/Rapho, top; Charles Harbutt/Magnum, bottom left; Ken Heyman, bottom right. page 41: Sandra Weiner, top right; Sherry Suris/Rapho, middle left; Henry Margulies, middle right; Pat Ross, bottom. page 42: Hella Hammid/Rapho.

This is a Borzoi Book Published by Alfred A. Knopf, Inc.

Copyright © 1975 by Betty Miles. All rights reserved under International and Pan-American Copyright Conventions. Published in the United States by Alfred A. Knopf, Inc., New York, and simultaneously in Canada by Random House of Canada Limited, Toronto. Distributed by Random House, Inc., New York. Library of Congress Cataloging in Publication Data Miles, Betty. Around and around—love. *Summary:* Text and photographs describe the many facets of love. 1. Love—Pictorial works. [1. Love—Pictorial works] I. Title. BF575.L8M45 1975 152.4 75-2539 ISBN 0-394-73137-9 ISBN 0-394-93111-4 lib. bdg.
Manufactured in the United States of America

for Matt

Love, love, love.

Given and found,

it's all around—

love.

It's hard to tell about,

easy to show.

Hugs and caring,

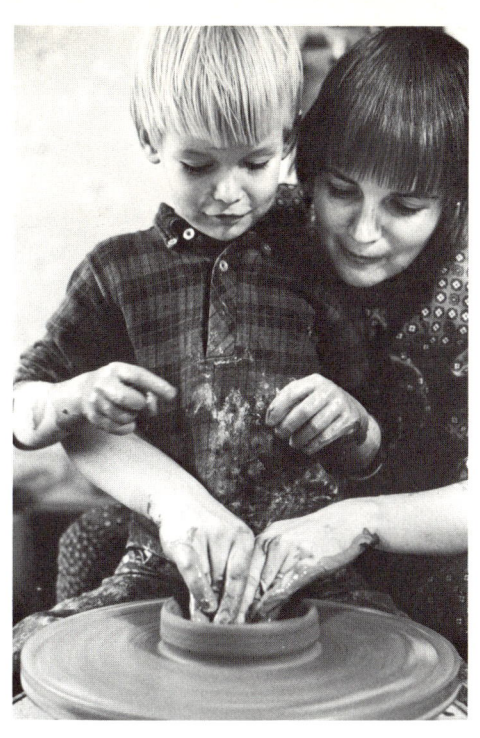
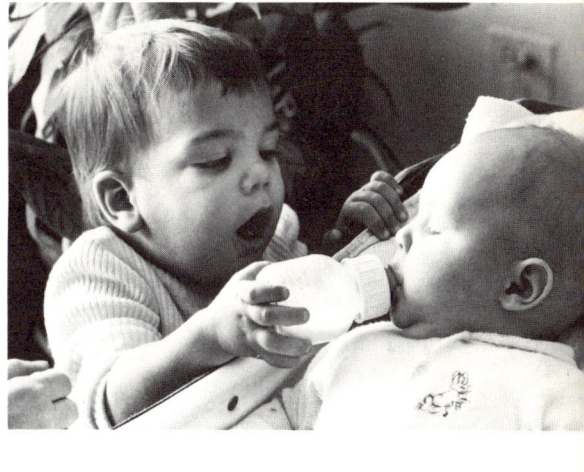

working and sharing are love.

You can't grab it or take it;
when you give it, you make it.

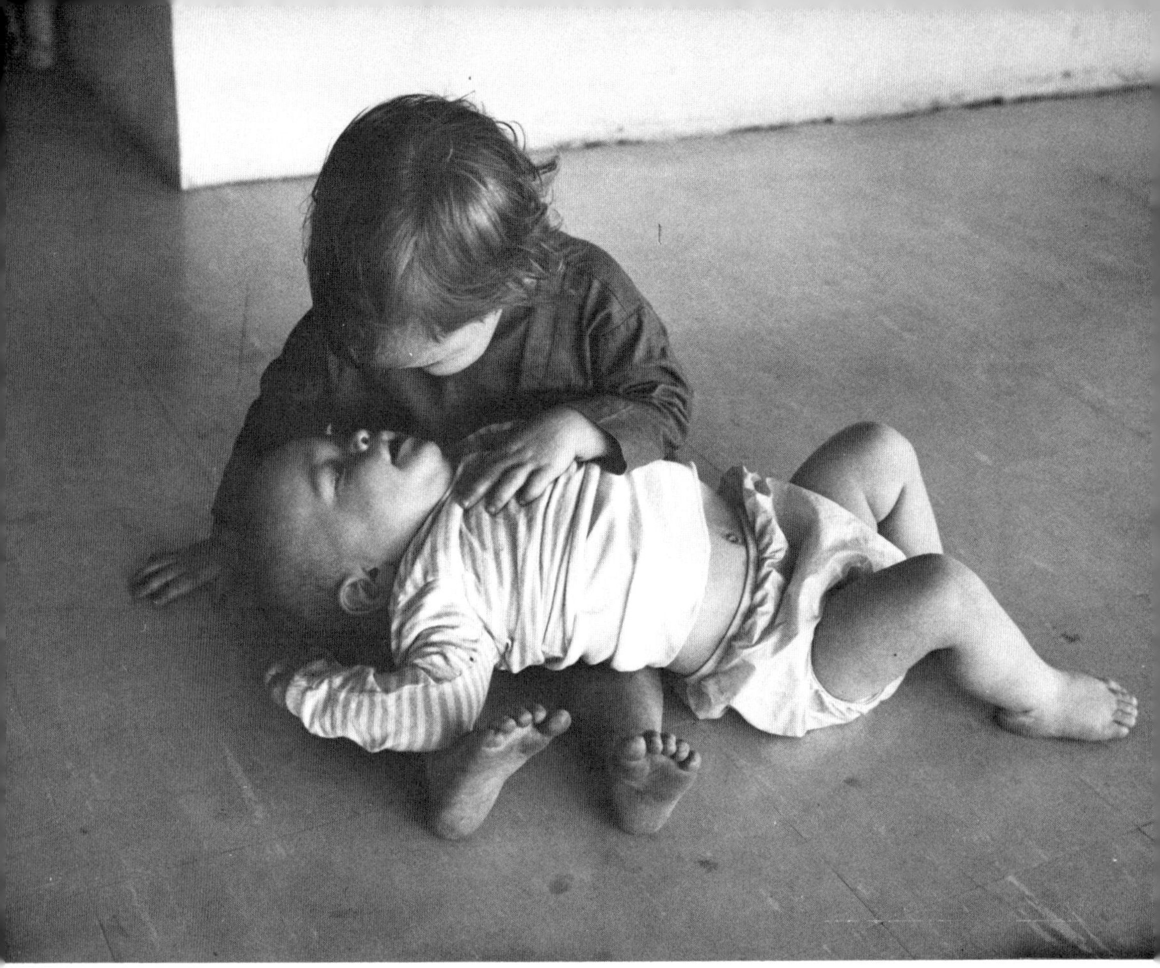

Love doesn't stay the same.
It changes as people change,
grows as people grow.

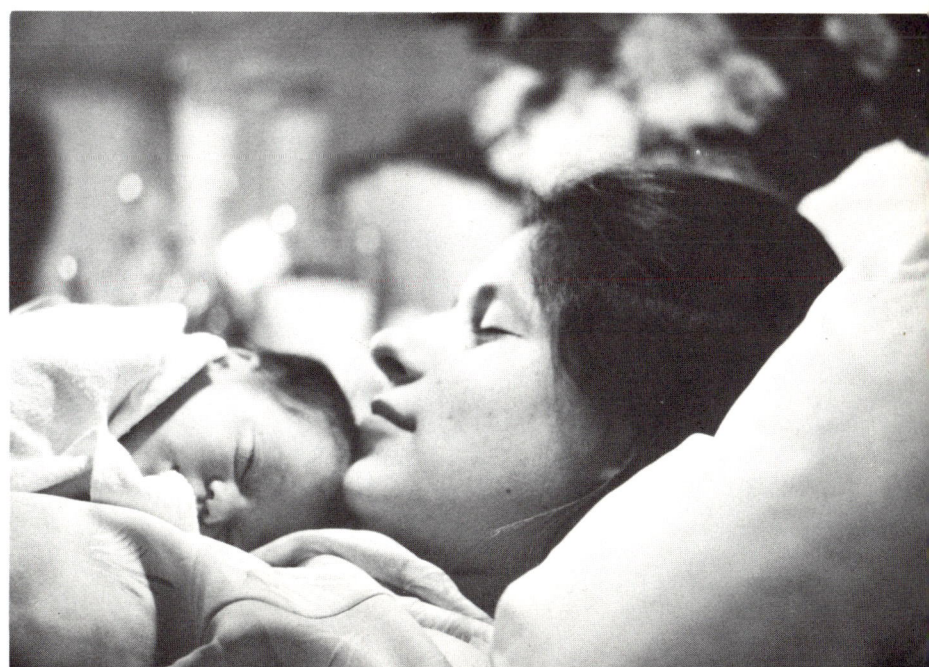

You can come
and go,

say goodbye
or hello,

hold – or let go. Love.

You can't
use it up.

Love is always around.

Like the sound
of the beat
of your heart,
like sun
in the sky,

love is part of your life till you die.

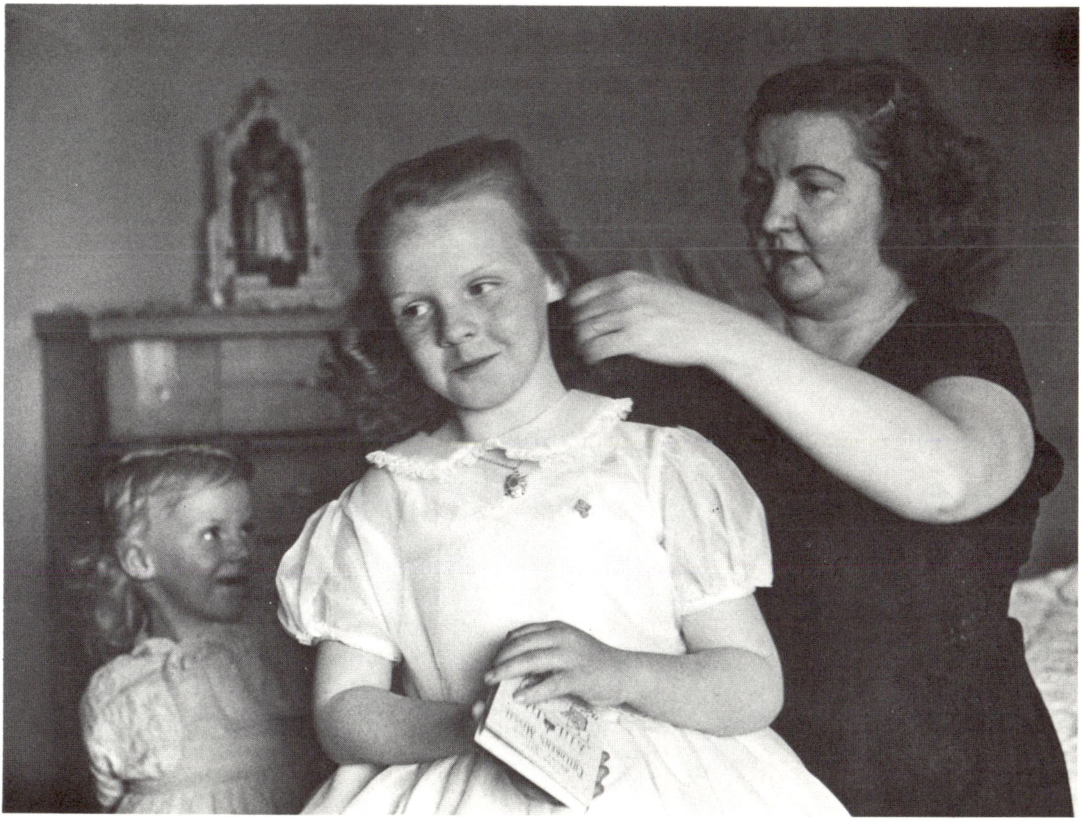

Love can make you feel so glad,
love is a comfort when you feel bad.

But love can
make you angry,

troubled
and sad.

Some people
don't believe it,
have to doubt it,
try to keep it
from their mind.

Most people find
that love is kind.

When you feel it and know it,

tell it and show it.

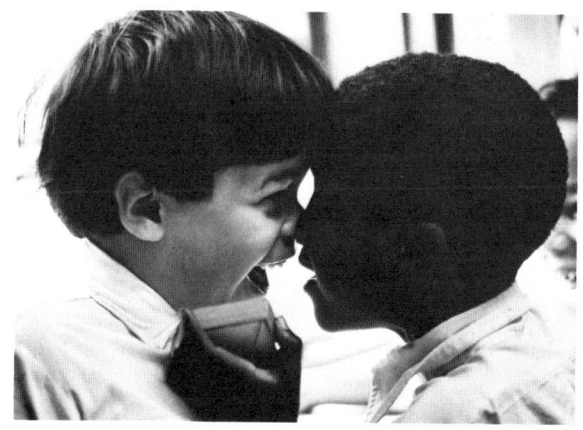

Whisper it, shout it,

feel good about it!

Given and found,

it's all around.

Around

and around

and around—

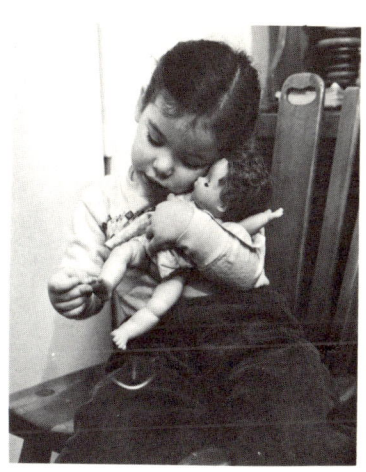

and around

love.